3-D THRILLERS!

D0672907

SHARKS
and the World's Scariest Sea Monsters

CHRIS COODE & LYNN GIBBONS

SCHOLASTIC

New York • Toronto • London • Auckland
Sydney • Mexico City • New Delhi • Hong Kong

MASTERS OF

Sharks have been swimming in the world's oceans for over 400 million years—that's 200 million years before the dinosaurs appeared! There are more than 400 different shark species, and still more are being discovered.

▼ Boneless fish

Most fish skeletons are made of bone, but sharks' skeletons are made of a tough, bendable material called *cartilage*—the same elastic material inside our ears and noses. Cartilage is flexible and lightweight, so sharks can twist and turn quickly when chasing prey.

THE DEEP

▶ Cousin ray

Although there may seem to be little family resemblance, the shark's closest relatives are rays, skates, and chimeras. Like their shark cousins, they also have skeletons of cartilage.

A shark's body is covered in tiny, toothlike SCALES called DENTICLES. Rub a shark's skin one way, and it feels smooth—rub it the opposite way, and it's rough like SANDPAPER!

NO ORDINARY

Sharks are the deadliest predators in the ocean. When they hunt, all their senses go to work. First, a shark may hear a sick or wounded creature struggling from more than a mile away. The shark picks up the prey's scent in the water and tracks it to its source.

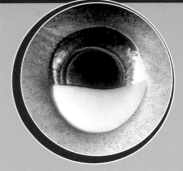

▲ Eye guard

When a shark thrashes around with struggling prey, the shark can get poked in the eye. To protect themselves, some shark species have a special eyelid called a *nictitating membrane* that covers the eye just before attack. Other sharks roll their eyes back into their heads.

Sixth sense ▶

A shark uses a special sense to pick up the electrical pulses that all living things give off. This "electro-sense" helps the shark pinpoint the exact location of its prey so it can strike with amazing accuracy.

Login accounts:

- **Symptom**   A previously disabled account or locked-out system accounts have been enabled, or unknown new accounts are identified.

- **Compromise**   The existence of previously disabled user accounts or system accounts such as (nobody) may indicate a system compromise. The attacker might be hiding his activities by masquerading as an end user. The existence of new, unknown user accounts may indicate that a Trojan horse program or rootkit has been run.

- **Investigation**   Review with your human resources department which accounts should be active.

On UNIX, the root account has a user ID of 0. If any other accounts have a user ID of 0, a compromise has occurred.

Group membership:

- **Symptom**   End users other than IT staff are included in administrative-level groups (for example, the wheel group on many types of UNIX, or the administrators group on Win32).

- **Compromise**   User group membership should always be as restrictive as possible. End user membership in administrative-level groups may indicate that a privilege escalation has occurred.

- **Investigation**   Review the /etc/passwd file in UNIX and the User manager in Win32. Review login audit logs to identify user login activity for the accounts in question.

User environment settings:

- **Symptom**   Modifications to administrative-level login environments (environment variables).

- **Compromise**   User environment variables define paths and user settings. Alterations to administrative-level account environment variables may indicate a compromise has occurred. For example, by altering the path variable, alternate versions of common programs can be run without the knowledge of the user.

- **Investigation**   In UNIX, run the env command to display environment variable values. In Win32, view environment variables from Computer Properties | Advanced.

Identifying a Compromise

File Systems/Volumes and Processes

A usual part of a system compromise is for one or more files to be replaced by modified versions, other hacking tools added, temporary files created, and permissions changed. Any or all of these can be a clear sign on its own but are often seen in conjunction with other factors listed here.

File checksum sweep:

- **Symptom**   Inconsistent file checksums are discovered.

- **Compromise**   Inconsistent file checksums may indicate that binaries have been replaced by Trojan horse programs.

- **Investigation**   Run file checksum sweeps on a regular basis and compare the results. The MD5 suite of utilities is an easy, inexpensive way of maintaining file checksums.

Maintaining file checksums requires a certain degree of discipline by the administrator. The task of regenerating file checksums after every system change requires additional administrative overhead. It may seem arduous, but it is the best way of keeping a baseline of changes made to a system. Without these checksums, the task of identifying a Trojan horse program will be significantly more difficult.

Presence of exploit tools:

- **Symptom**   Password cracking software, keystroke loggers, network packet sniffers, or other exploit tools are discovered.

- **Compromise**   Attackers often upload attack scripts, tools, and rootkits.

- **Investigation**   Periodic file system sweeps should be performed to look for the existence of common exploit tool binaries. This task can be incorporated into the periodic checksum sweeps.

Altered application output:

- **Symptom**   A command that once ran now results in an error or somewhat different output.

- **Compromise**   A common Trojan horse program technique is to alter standard system commands to hide unauthorized activity. Many Trojan horse programs, however, also slightly modify the output of the command.

- **Investigation**   Perform a file checksum sweep to identify files that have changed.

HUNTERS

A shark's body shape helps make it a champion PREDATOR. Most sharks have a torpedo-shaped body, which allows them to glide smoothly—and swiftly—through the water after their prey.

GRABBING H

The dinner menu is quite similar for most kinds of sharks. They prefer smaller fish (including other sharks) and invertebrates such as squid. Large sharks, such as the great white and the bull shark, also feed on marine mammals. Sharks often prey on sick or wounded animals, since they are easier to catch.

▲ Dental care

Every time a shark eats, some of its teeth break or fall out. Luckily, replacement teeth from the row behind are waiting to take their places. Some sharks have 10 or more rows of teeth and go through over 20,000 teeth in a lifetime!

◄ Take a bite

One of the weirdest feeders of all is the cookie-cutter shark. Its round mouth is specially designed to take cookie-sized bites out of larger animals, such as whales and dolphins. However, its "cookie bites" are not fatal to its victims.

BITE

In just ONE hour, the basking shark, shown above, can FILTER enough water to fill a large swimming pool!

▲ Filter feeders

The largest sharks in the ocean—the whale shark, the megamouth, and the basking shark—eat some of the smallest food! Their mouths act like giant strainers to filter tiny plants, called *plankton*, out of the water.

UNLIKE THE

The many different shark species come in a huge variety of sizes and shapes. The biggest, the whale shark, can grow more than 50 feet (15 m) long, while the smallest, the pygmy shark, is only 9 inches (23 cm) long.

▲ Spots or stripes?

Baby zebra sharks have black and yellow stripes, but as the sharks grow, the markings change into pale brown spots. The adults are therefore sometimes called leopard sharks.

◄ Funny face

Hammerhead sharks are easy to recognize! Their eyes sit on either side of their broad, T-shaped heads and give them excellent all-around vision. Hammerheads use their heads to pin stingrays and other prey to the ocean floor!

REST

▲ Hornshark

The hornshark gets its name from the two sharp spines that stick out from its dorsal fins. The spines make predators think twice before attacking. This 3.3-foot (1 m) shark lives on the ocean bottom off the coast of California and Mexico.

▼ Spot the shark

Many bottom-dwelling sharks, such as this tasselled wobbegong, are covered in spots, blotches, or stripes so that they blend in with the seabed. This helps them hide from enemies and catch unsuspecting prey.

THE HEAVY

In this corner, the most infamous shark in the ocean—the great white. In the far corner, the largest shark in the world, known as the "gentle giant"—the whale shark. How do these shark heavyweights measure up?

▼ Great white

Scientific name: *Carcharodon carcharias*

Size: Also known as "white death" or "white pointer," this is the largest flesh-eating shark. It is about 20 feet (6 m) long and weighs over 2 tons.

Coloring: Its upper body is blue-gray and its underbody is lighter, sometimes even white.

Range: The great white lives in cool waters in subtropical and temperate seas.

Diet: With its 2-inch (5 cm) serrated teeth, it eats fish and sea mammals such as seals and sea lions.

HITTERS

A shark's JAWS are not connected to its skull, so it can open its mouth REALLY wide!

▲ Whale shark

Scientific name: *Rhincodon typus*

Size: Measuring over 50 feet (15 m) long and weighing more than 13 tons, the whale shark is the largest shark, and the largest fish, in the world.

Coloring: On top it is blue-gray, but underneath it is white. Its skin is camouflaged with distinctive white spots and bars to help it blend in with the surrounding water.

Range: The whale shark lives in warm waters on either side of the equator, both in the open ocean and near the shore.

Diet: The shark flushes huge mouthfuls of water over its *gill rakers* (walls of spongy mesh inside its throat). The gill rakers act as a sieve, trapping plankton for the shark to swallow.

SHARKS VS.

Despite the scary attacks you may have seen at the movies, shark attacks on humans are rare. There are only about 50 attacks reported each year. The "usual suspects" are the tiger, bull, great white, and oceanic whitetip sharks. But sharks are much more threatened by humans than we are by them.

▼ My mistake

Many shark attacks on humans are a case of mistaken identity. To a shark, a diver wearing a wet suit and flippers, or a surfer on a surfboard, can look like one of its favorite foods—a seal or a sea turtle.

MAN

▲ Pollution

Sharks mature slowly and give birth to few young. Often they are killed by pollution or overfishing more quickly than they can reproduce. Pollution kills the fish they eat and also destroys breeding grounds.

▲ Human attack!

The truth is, people are far more dangerous to sharks than they are to us. Every year we catch 100 million sharks for their meat, skin, teeth, oil, and fins, and sometimes just for fun. Many sharks are also accidentally caught in nets meant for other fish.

◄ Tacky souvenirs

Sharks are also killed for their jaws, which are sold as souvenirs. Tourists should think about the source of those jaws before they consider buying them.

DOWN IN THE

Sharks aren't the only scary creatures in the sea. The oceans are home to some of the strangest animals you could imagine—and many of the most weird are found at the very bottom of the sea, where it's cold, dark, and dangerous.

▼ Luring them in

The female anglerfish uses a glowing ball of light hanging from its dorsal fin to attract small fish, like an angler with a baited hook. When the prey gets too close, the anglerfish suddenly springs to life and gulps down the hapless victim.

◄ Fang-tastic

Some of the scariest teeth to be found in the ocean belong to the viperfish—they're so big they can't even fit inside the fish's mouth. The fish is only 10 inches (25 cm), so it's not a real threat to larger fish.

DARK

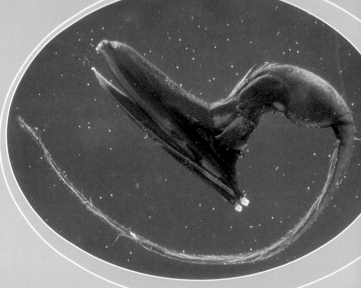

▲ Jeepers creepers

The Greenland shark's shining eyes make it look more menacing than it really is—it's actually quite a harmless creature. This rare shark is one of the few that live in Arctic waters. It is also one of the largest sharks. The light in its eyes is not produced by the fish itself, but by a parasite that lives on the poor shark's peepers.

Big mouth ▶

The gulper eel has two big advantages for a deep-sea predator—a huge mouth and an expanding stomach. The gulper eel's large mouth can swallow prey as big as the eel itself. Fortunately, this eel's stomach can stretch just as much to accommodate a sizable lunch!

THE ANCIENT

L ife developed in the seas long
before it did on land, so it'll come
as no surprise that there were
some pretty scary creatures floating
around our oceans in the past. Here
is a selection of the top underwater
predators of the prehistoric world.

▼ Snap, snap!

Today's largest crocodile—the estuarine,
or saltwater, crocodile—grows over
20 feet (6 m) in length. This is
impressive, but it's tiny compared to its
ancient relatives. Some early crocodiles
measured up to 40 feet (12 m).

SEAS

Toothless ▶ terror

Over 360 million years ago, one fish not to be messed with was *Dunkleosteus* (dun-kul-OS-tee-us). At around 20 feet (6 m) long, this armor-plated monster was bigger than today's great white shark. Instead of teeth, each jaw had a hard, bony edge—just right for crunching anything that came swimming by!

▼ Nessie

One of the most famous (but maybe mythical) monsters in the world is Nessie, rumored to inhabit a lake in Scotland called Loch Ness. It is said that Nessie is a living plesiosaur (PLE-zee-oh-sore). Nessie spotters report seeing a creature with a long neck and a humpback, which is how a plesiosaur looked!

TALL

L egens of sea monsters have been told for centuries. Seafarers, who had been at sea for months on end, often returned to shore with frightening tales of mysterious creatures. There must be something terrifying about being at the sea's mercy that plays tricks on the mind!

▼ To boldly go

Centuries ago, sailing was a dangerous experience. Battling stormy seas in wooden ships meant that the threat of being shipwrecked was ever present. Explorers pushed the boundaries of the known world farther and farther—and with this came the natural fear of the unknown. Sailors' imaginations ran wild!

TALES!

Strange world ▶

Many stories about sea monsters were not written down by sailors but by ships' passengers, who could afford education and travel. Imagine seeing a giant squid and not knowing what it was! Scholars who wrote of sea monsters may not even have been to sea themselves, but were merely recounting tales that had been told to them.

▲ Scare stories

Sometimes, stories of sea monsters were used just for entertainment. But some early traders deliberately spread scary rumors as a way of discouraging others from following their highly profitable trade routes.

SERPENTS

The classic sea monster is, of course, the sea serpent. There have been reports of gigantic snakelike creatures in the oceans for hundreds of years. However, many of the most famously reported giant serpents come from large inland lakes around the world. So what's the real story?

▼ Monster fame

As well as Nessie from Loch Ness, the world's famous serpentlike monsters include Ogopogo from Lake Okanagan in Canada, Champ from Lake Champlain on the eastern US-Canadian border, and Chessie from the Chesapeake Bay on the east coast of the United States.

◀ Fabulous fish

One kind of sea serpent does exist. Don't believe it? Well, check out exhibit A, the oarfish. At around 30 feet (9 m) long, the oarfish looks unlike any other species of fish. Could this unusual creature be what sailors have been mistaking for a sea serpent all this time?

▼ Snakes alive

Of course, there are real snakes that swim in the sea, too. Some sea snakes have flattened bodies, which help them swim but also make them look rather odd. Is it possible that reports of the river-dwelling anaconda of South America—which grows over 30 feet (9 m) in length—have convinced people that similar monsters live in the ocean?

SUCKERED IN

Take a peek at an octopus or a squid. The rubbery texture and all those suckery legs writhing around like a nest of snakes are enough to give most people nightmares. Imagine seeing a gigantic squid coming at you while you are out for a swim!

◀ Kraken

The most famous of the mythical squidlike monsters was the Kraken. There have been many tales of this giant creature coming out of the sea and dragging boats down beneath the waves. It was claimed that the Kraken was as big as an island!

▲ Ancient tales

Seafarers have long told tales of giant octopuses and squid attacking ships. These stories have made it into literature—most famously in Jules Verne's *Twenty Thousand Leagues Under the Sea*. There's also a legend that a type of octopus, nicknamed Lusca, lives in the Caribbean and grows to 132 feet (40 m) long! But there's little real proof.

Real-life monster ▶

The closest thing to the Kraken that we know of is the giant squid. Some scientists estimate that it can grow up to 60 feet (18 m) long; that's about the length of a bus. There is some evidence, however, of a colossal squid that could be twice the size of the giant squid—that's a lot of calamari!

SWHLLOWEU

The terrible fear of being eaten alive by a hungry shark, or even by an angry sea monster, is the subject of many films, books, and tall tales. But how likely is it that a person could really be swallowed up by an underwater predator?

▼ Deadly taster

Undoubtedly, sharks such as the great white and the tiger shark do occasionally attack people, but humans aren't their favorite food. Most attacks happen when the shark has a quick taste, but then abandons its victim when it realizes that it's not the type of snack it wants.

WHOLE

There is a TALE that in the 1890s, a sailor called James Bartley was SWALLOWED alive by a sperm whale and survived for 15 hours in the whale's stomach!

▲ Big fish

Could you be eaten by a basking shark or a whale shark? They are the two biggest types of fish in the sea, but these two sharks eat tiny sea creatures and aren't very likely to swallow a human.

Tiny food ▶

Although whales look big enough to eat a human, many of them actually eat small sea creatures called *krill*. They trap the krill in comblike plates of bone, called *baleen*, in their mouths. Other whales have teeth. The biggest of these toothed whales is the sperm whale.

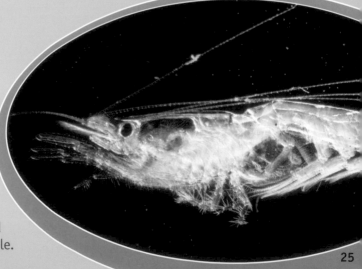

WHAT IS IT?

T he only way to tell for sure exactly what lives in the ocean is to go out and look for it. Unfortunately, that's easier said than done. There's a lot of water out there—it covers over 71 percent of the planet.

▼ Megasurprise

We can be fairly sure that there are some big animals out there still waiting to be found. No one knew that the megamouth shark existed until 1976, when one was caught accidentally by a research vessel off the coast of Hawaii. If this 16-foot (5 m) shark could stay hidden until recently, then what else is out there?

◄ Scientists or not?

The practice of looking for animals considered to be either mythical or extinct is called *cryptozoology*. Many people criticize cryptozoologists, saying that they're not actual scientists.

▼ Hide-and-seek

Most of the sea remains unexplored, mainly because it's difficult to study such a large area. Also, the seabed isn't nice and flat. Instead it's made up of mountains and trenches that are miles deep, so there are plenty of places for large and unusual creatures, such as this giant manta ray, to hide.

PROTECTING

ach year, many sharks are killed by overfishing or by polluted waters. Several kinds, including the great white, blue, and basking sharks, are in trouble. They are classified as threatened species, meaning their numbers are dwindling so rapidly that they could be in danger of dying out. If shark species died out, all ocean life would suffer.

◄ What is being done?

Marine biologists and conservation groups are working hard to make sure we don't hunt sharks to extinction. Biologists study sharks in their natural environment to learn more about their behavior. Conservation groups pressure governments to pass laws to protect sharks, and set up underwater nature reserves where sharks can live without danger of being fished by humans. The more we know about sharks, the more we can do to help save them.

▼ Cleaning up the ocean

Sharks are at the top of the ocean food chain. This means that they don't have any predators (except each other)—sharks are the animals that prey on others. As predators, they keep many fish populations in check. They also act as scavengers, eating up dead animals and helping to keep the ocean clean.

FUN FACTS!

Now that you've had a quick swim through the world of sharks and sea monsters, maybe you think you know it all? Well, here are a few amazing facts to turn you into a real undersea expert!

▼ Greedy tiger!

The tiger shark is known for its greedy habits. Some of the more unusual "foods" found in its stomach include car license plates, shoes, weights, tin cans, and an alarm clock!

The fastest shark is the SHORTFIN MAKO. It can swim up to 46 miles per hour (74 kph) in short bursts. That's twice the speed of the fastest human on record!

▲ Up close and scary

People are willing to pay a lot of money to see a great white shark up close. Tourists can take part in cage-diving expeditions, during which they are lowered into the water inside a big cage, hoping to experience the thrill of seeing a massive shark glide past!

Mmm ... dinner!

Some types of shark can smell a single drop of blood in the water from nearly half a mile away. The best sniffers, for instance the nurse shark, have fleshy whiskers called BARBELS on their noses, which greatly improve their ability to track prey.

This edition created in 2010 by
Arcturus Publishing Limited, 26/27 Bickels Yard,
151–153 Bermondsey Street, London SE1 3HA

Copyright © 2010 by Arcturus Publishing Limited

All rights reserved. Published by Scholastic Inc.,
Publishers since 1920. SCHOLASTIC and associated
logos are trademarks and/or registered trademarks
of Scholastic Inc.

No part of this publication may be reproduced,
stored in a retrieval system, or transmitted
in any form or by any means, electronic,
mechanical, photocopying, recording, or
otherwise, without written permission of the
publisher. For information regarding permission,
write to Scholastic Inc., Attention: Permissions
Department, 557 Broadway, New York, NY 10012.

ISBN 978-0-545-21849-8

10 9 8   12 13 14

Printed in Malaysia 106

First Scholastic edition, June 2010

ARCTURUS CREDITS
Authors: Chris Coode and Lynn Gibbons
Editors: Jacqueline McCann and Lisa Miles
Designers: Beatriz Reis Custodio and Mike Reynolds
Illustrator (glasses): Ian Thompson

PICTURE CREDITS
BBC: p. 2, p. 3 top, p. 4 top, p. 6 top,
  p. 7, p. 8 bottom, p. 10
Bridgeman Art Library: p. 18
Chris Harvey-Clark: p. 15 top
Getty Images: front cover
Jamie Oliver: p. 28 top
Natural History Museum: p. 17 top and
  bottom, back cover left
NHPA: p. 15 bottom, p. 16, p. 25 bottom,
  p. 27 bottom
Nature Picture Library: p. 14 top and bottom,
  p. 21 bottom, p. 23 bottom, p. 24, p. 26

Oxford Scientific Films: p. 1, p. 3 middle,
  pp. 4–5 bottom, p. 5 top, p. 6 bottom,
  p. 8 top, p. 11, p. 12, p. 13 top right,
  p. 13 bottom, p. 31
Planet Earth: p. 9 top and bottom, p. 13 top
  left, p. 28 bottom, p. 29
Science Photo Library: p. 19 bottom, p. 20,
  p. 23 top, p. 27 top
Shutterstock: p. 25 top, p. 30, back cover right
Topfoto: p. 19 top, p. 21 top, p. 22

3-D images produced by Pinsharp